THE
ARSENAL
COLLECTION

T H E
ARSENAL
COLLECTION

breedon **books**
PUBLISHING

First published in Great Britain in 2003 by
The Breedon Books Publishing Company Limited
Breedon House, 3 The Parker Centre,
Derby, DE21 4SZ.

ISBN 1 85983 390 X

Printed and bound by Butler & Tanner,
Frome, Somerset, England.

Cover printing by Lawrence-Allen Colour Printers,
Weston-super-Mare, Somerset, England.

Contents

Introduction

IT was at a meeting held at the Prince of Wales public house in Plumstead in October 1886 that some football enthusiasts from the north formed the football club that would one day be one of the most famous in the world. They called in Dial Square FC, after the workshop where they were all employed at the Woolwich Arsenal munitions factory. Two months later they played their first match and beat Eastern Wanderers 6-0 at Millwall. It was an auspicious start.

Before Christmas, the men had changed the name of their club. Again they met in a pub, this time the Royal Oak in Woolwich, where they decided that henceforth their fledgling club should be known as Royal Arsenal. Thus, in January 1887 they played their first game under that name, against Erith on Plumstead Common, where they won 6-1. The next game saw Alexandria United beaten 11-0. By the end of their first season, Royal Arsenal had played ten matches, all friendlies, and won seven of them, scoring 36 goals on the way and conceding only eight.

For their second season of 1887-88, the club rented the Sportsman's Ground on Plumstead Marshes and entered their first competition, the London Senior Cup, where they were beaten by Barnes in the second round.

People were now flocking to see the club and for 1888-89, Arsenal rented the Manor Ground in Plumstead, and in 1889-90 entered the FA Cup for the first time. They reached the last qualifying round before losing 5-1 to Swifts, and in the London Senior Cup they got to the Final where Old Westminsters beat them. It was not an entirely unsuccessful season, however, and at its end Arsenal could parade the London Charity Cup, the Kent Senior Cup and the Kent Junior Cup.

Season 1890-91 saw another change of home venue, this time to the Invicta Ground in Plumstead.

The club was now really making progress, excused the qualifying rounds of the FA Cup and chalking up successes in several other cup competitions. In the summer of 1893 they changed their name again – to Woolwich Arsenal – and became a limited liability company. They also returned to the Manor Ground, which they bought outright and which remained their home until they moved to Highbury in 1913. Finally, in September 1893, Arsenal became a Football League club, joining the newly-enlarged Second Division. Their first League game was a 2-2 home draw against Newcastle United, also newly-elected.

In 1903-04, Arsenal finished runners-up to Preston North End and were promoted to the top flight of English football. Those days were fraught with difficulties, however, and in 1912 the

Gunners were relegated with one of the worst playing records ever seen in League football. Worse, they were in dire financial straits and it was only the intervention of Henry Norris, chairman of Fulham, which kept them alive.

It was Norris who took the club to Highbury in 1913. Not surprisingly, since they now played in North London, the 'Woolwich' part of their name was finally dropped before World War One. After the war, the Football League decided to extend the First Division by two clubs and Arsenal, although they had finished fifth in 1914-15, were promoted. It was a highly controversial move by the League and one club who could rightly feel aggrieved were Tottenham Hotspur, who had finished bottom of the First Division in the last post-war season; they were still relegated.

The first six seasons of the inter-war years brought no success – and a flirtation with relegation once more – but in the summer of 1925, Huddersfield Town's manager Herbert Chapman took over at Highbury. It was at that moment that the Arsenal we all know today was born.

In his first season Chapman steered the Gunners to the last eight of the FA Cup and to runners-up spot in the First Division. In 1927 they reached their first FA Cup Final, where they lost to Cardiff City, and three years later won the trophy for the first time .

That 1930 Wembley success signalled the start of a remarkable era for Arsenal. The following season they became the first southern club to win the Football League championship – and with a record number of points – and from 1932-33 they won three consecutive League titles. Sadly, Herbert Chapman died in January 1934. The hat-trick of championships was completed under George Allison's managership. In the FA Cup, Arsenal lost the 1932 Final but won the Cup again in 1936. In 1937-38 came a fifth League championship in eight seasons.

After World War Two yet another title was added, in 1947-48, and another FA Cup Final triumph came in 1950. And the early 1950s, continued in that vein: an appearance in the 1952 Cup Final and a seventh League title in 1953, Coronation Year.

That, however, was the highlight for the rest of the 1950s, and indeed for most of the 60s. Not until 1968, did Arsenal get anywhere near another trophy. That year they lost 1-0 to Leeds in the League Cup Final, and a year later were beaten in the Final of the same competition by Third Division Swindon Town. Those last few years had been some of the most disappointing in Arsenal's history.

But in just two short years, the Gunners' fortunes changed dramatically and in 1971 they won the League and Cup double. It was a success of almost mythical proportions, and emulated Tottenham's feat of ten years earlier. Later in the 1970s, there were more FA Cup Finals, and European success too.

Our story covers this era, from the days at Plumstead in the early years of the last century, right up to the 1971 double and beyond.

Plumstead to Highbury

Woolwich Arsenal, 1900-01. Back row (left to right): Dr Clark (chairman), F. Warman (assistant trainer), Fred Coles, Duncan McNichol, Andy Main, Tom Spicer, Jimmy Jackson, Walter Place, J. Hindle (trainer), Harry Bradshaw (manager). Middle row: Tom Low, John Dick, John Blackwood, Peter Turner, James Tennant. Front row: Alex McCowie, John Anderson, Tom Grieve. This season Arsenal finished seventh in Division Two and were knocked out of the FA Cup by West Brom.

Woolwich Arsenal in 1905-06. Back row (left to right): R.Dunmore (trainer), James Sharp, James Ashcroft, Percy Sands, Archie Cross, Philip Kelso (manager). Middle row: Archie Gray, Bobby Templeton, Andy Ducat, Tom Fitchie, Roddie McEachrane. Front row: James Bellamy, John Dick, James Blair. They finished 12th in Division One and reached the FA Cup semi-final where they lost to Newcastle United at Stoke.

Woolwich Arsenal defend their goal against Sheffield Wednesday at Plumstead in November 1905. A 20,000 crowd saw the Owls win 2-0.

Action from the FA Cup quarter-final match between Woolwich Arsenal and Manchester United at Bank Street, Clayton, in March 1906 when 26,500 saw the Gunners win 3-2.

Aerial action from the game between Woolwich Arsenal and Bristol City at Plumstead in September 1907. It was the second game of the First Division season and Arsenal were thumped 4-0.

A view from behind the Manor Ground goal as Woolwich Arsenal attack the Bristol City goal.

Two weeks later, Manchester City were beaten 2-1 at Plumstead as the Gunners recovered from their poor start to the 1907-08 season.

Woolwich Arsenal, 1908-09. Back row (left to right): John Dick, David Greenaway, Roddie McEachrane, Billy Curle. Middle row: Archie Gray, Hugh McDonald, Joe Shaw, Andy Ducat, Archie Cross, Sam Raybould, Percy Sands. Front row: Charlie Lewis, Charlie Satterthwaite, Harry Lee, David Neave.

Woolwich Arsenal's Peter Kyle heads towards the Hull City goal during the first-round FA Cup tie at the Manor Ground in January 1908. The games finished goalless but Hull won the replay 4–1.

Heads high at Ashton Gate in January 1909 where Woolwich Arsenal and Bristol City drew 1–1.

Arsenal in 1911-12. Back row (left to right): John Peart, John Grant, Joe Shaw, George Burdett, Harry Crawford, Archie Gray, David Neave. Middle row: A.Keard (honorary secretary), G.Hardy (trainer), Fred Calvert, E.Gatenby. Andy Ducat, Matt Thomson, Percy Sands (captain), Alf Common, Charlie Lewis, Willis Rippon, J.Humble (director), John Dick (coach and assistant trainer). Front row: John Flanagan, Angus McKinnon, Les Calder, John Chalmers, George Morrell (manager-secretary), Tom Winship, David Greenaway, Pip Rippon, Roddie McEachrane. At the end of the season Arsenal were 10th in Division One. They went out of the FA Cup at the first hurdle, to Bolton.

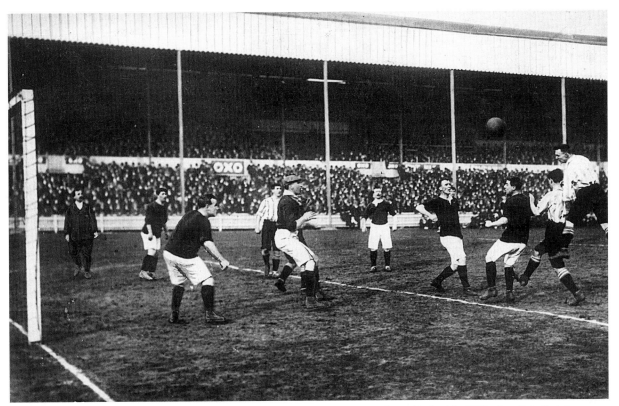

Sheffield Wednesday attack the Woolwich Arsenal goal during a match at the Manor Ground before World War One. Note that the Arsenal goalkeeper (wearing cap) is not wearing a distinguishing jersey.

Jack Cock is too late as Spurs' goalkeeper, Fred Hinton, grabs the ball on the opening day of 1925-26.

In July 1925, Arsenal signed Sunderland's England international forward Charlie Buchan for £2,000 plus £100 a goal; that rider cost the Gunners another £5,600, as Buchan hit 56 League and Cup goals in 120 senior appearances before he retired in May 1928. The Gunners, though, could have had him for nothing. Plumstead-born Buchan had been on their books in 1909 but they let him go to Leyton. When he returned via Wearside, he was one of the game's major figures and a war hero as well, having won the Military Medal in World War One.

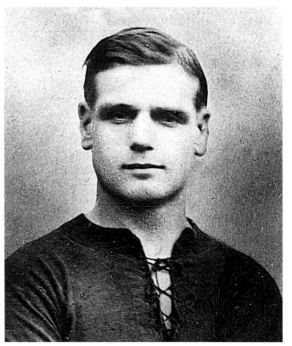

Jock Rutherford joined Arsenal from Newcastle for £800 in October 1913. He joined Stoke as manager in April 1923 but five months later returned to Arsenal as a player. An outside-right, Rutherford made 232 League and FA Cup appearances for the Gunners.

Alf Baker, a unility player, joined Arsenal in May 1919 after guesting for several League clubs in wartime. He retired at the end of the 1930-31 season, after 351 League and FA Cup appearances.

Charlie Buchan (far right) in a battle for the ball with Tottenham's Forster and Clay at Highbury in December 1926. Nearly 50,000 saw the Gunners go down 4-2.

A balletic scene – albeit with no sign of the ball – from the FA Cup quarter-final game between Arsenal and Wolves at Highbury in March 1927. Charlie Buchan is the only Gunners player in view.

A fumble from the Wolves goalkeeper Noel George as Buchan races in. Arsenal won the tie 2-1 and were a step nearer to their first FA Cup Final.

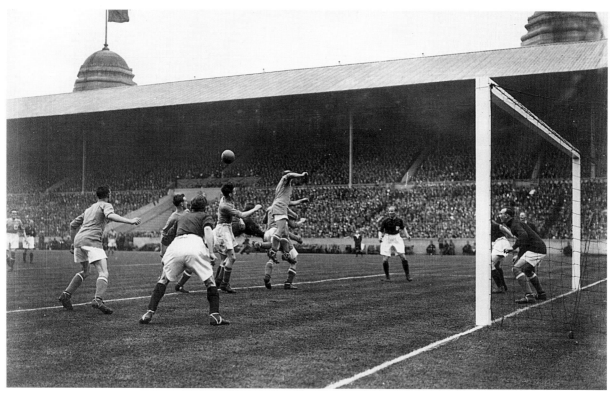

Cardiff City clear the ball from an Arsenal attack in the 1927 FA Cup Final.

One of the most famous goals in FA Cup Final history. Arsenal's Dan Lewis lets a long shot from Hughie Ferguson slip under his body and out of his grasp and Cardiff City are on their way to an historic victory at Wembley in 1927.

Arsenal clear the ball from West Brom attackers in the third-round FA Cup tie at Highbury in January 1928. The Gunners won 2-0 to set up a fourth-round tie against Everton.

West Brom's goalkeeper George Ashmore dives on the ball but eventually Brain and Hulme put Arsenal through to the next round

Jimmy Brain has just scored Arsenal's first goal in the FA Cup fourth-round game against Everton at Highbury in January 1928. The Gunners went on to reach the semi-finals where they were beaten by Blackburn Rovers at Filbert Street.

Arsenal goalkeeper Dan Lewis collects the ball on a quagmire of a Highbury pitch. Dixie Dean is the Everton centre-forward rushing in to the right of the picture.

Everton goalkeeper Ted Taylor punches clear from an Arsenal attack.

Arsenal goalkeeper Dan Lewis knocks up the ball from an Aston Villa attack in the fifth-round FA Cup game at Highbury in February 1928. The Gunners won 4-1.

Police and ambulance men help spectators injured in the crush of bodies at the Villa Cup game.

An attendance of over 58,000 packed Highbury to watch the Cup game against Aston Villa. Here police officers help young boys to the front of the huge crowd.

In the quarter-finals of the 1927-28 FA Cup, Arsenal beat Stoke City 4-1. Here, the Gunners' defence look back at their own goal as Stoke attack.

Charlie Buchan looks on as Arsenal's Jimmy Brain is forced over the Stoke goal-line with the ball.

Arsenal supporters parade around Highbury before the game against Stoke.

Charlie Buchan puts the Blackburn Rovers goalkeeper under pressure during the 1928 FA Cup semi-final at Filbert Street. The Gunners lost 1-0, their hopes of a second successive Wembley appearance ended.

Mansfield Town's goalkeeper Staples punches clear from an Arsenal attack in the fourth-round FA Cup game at Highbury in January 1929. The Gunners beat Mansfield, who were then in the Midland League, 2-0, and eventually reached the quarter-finals where they lost 1-0 to Aston Villa.

The Glorious Thirties

The Arsenal team which lost 5-2 at Villa Park in September 1929. Back row (left to right): Len Thompson, unknown, Herbie Roberts, Charlie Preedy, Bill Seddon, Tom Whittaker (trainer), Jack Lambert. Front row: Joe Hulme, David Jack, Tom Parker, Alex James, Joe Williams, Eddie Hapgood.

The Arsenal team which beat Birmingham 3-2 at St Andrew's in November 1929. Back row (left to right): Alf Baker, Alex James, Dan Lewis, Herbie Roberts, Bob John. Front row: Joe Hulme, David Jack, David Halliday, Tom Parker, Charlie Jones, Eddie Hapgood. At the end of the season, the Gunners finished 14th but won the FA Cup.

Some of the 55,579 crowd pouring into Highbury for the third-round FA Cup game against Chelsea in January 1930. The Gunners won 2-0.

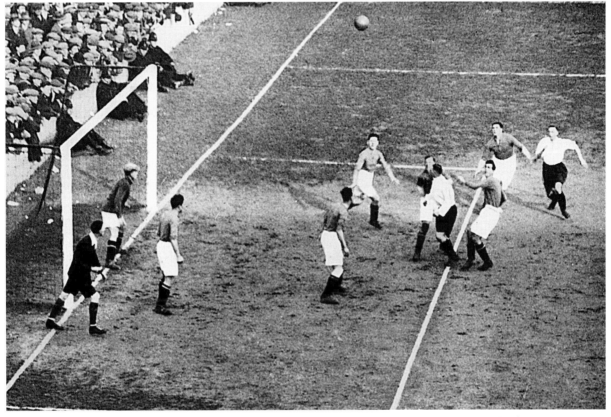

West Ham defend a corner against Arsenal during the quarter-final FA Cup match at Upton Park in March 1930. The Gunners won 3-0.

Arsenal on the defensive in the 1930 FA Cup semi-final against Second Division Hull City at Leeds Road, Huddersfield. The game at Elland Road ended 2-2.

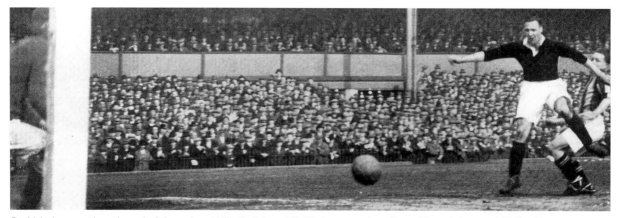

David Jack scores the only goal of the replay at Villa Park to end Hull's dreams and put Arsenal into their second FA Cup Final.

Arsenal skipper Tom Parker and Huddersfield's Tommy Wilson shake hands before the 1930 FA Cup Final.

Aerial battle between Arsenal and Huddersfield at Wembley. Alex James (centre, eyes shut) scored one of the goals, Jack Lambert the other, as the Gunners triumphed 2-0.

The Huddersfield defence is left grounded after James's goal put Arsenal ahead in the 16th minute.

A strange Cup Final visitor, the German airship the *Graf Zeppelin*, flies over Wembley.

Arsenal skipper Tom Parker clutches the FA Cup after the Gunners' victory over Huddersfield. Goalkeeper Charlie Preedy has a smile on his face but Bill Seddon and Joe Hulme look more reflective.

Arsenal with the FA Cup in 1930. Back row (left to right): Alf Baker, Jack Lambert, Charlie Preedy, Bill Seddon, Eddie Hapgood, Bob John. Middle row: Herbert Chapman (manager), David Jack, Tom Parker, Alex James, Tom Whittaker (trainer). Front row: Joe Hulme, Cliff Bastin.

Arsenal's Bill Harper cannot prevent Chelsea scoring their second goal in the fourth-round FA Cup tie at Stamford Bridge in January 1931. The Gunners went down 2-1.

Charlie Preedy collects the ball as Tom Parker covers, with Villa forward Billy Walker on the prowl in October 1931. The sides drew 1-1 at Highbury.

David Jack heads towards the Newcastle goal during the 1932 FA Cup Final. Arsenal lost 2-1.

Arsenal goalkeeper Frank Moss grabs the ball as a Newcastle forward races in. Herbie Roberts is on hand.

Arsenal pictured in the 1932-33 season. Back row (left to right): Tom Parker, Charlie Jones, Frank Moss, Herbie Roberts, Bob John, Tom Black. Front row: Herbert Chapman (manager), Joe Hulme, David Jack, Jack Lambert, Alex James, Cliff Bastin, Tom Whittaker (trainer). At the end of the season, the Gunners were champions, the first of three successive title successes.

Leicester City goalkeeper Joe Calvert races out to pick the ball off David Jack's foot at Highbury in October 1932. Arsenal won 8-2. The following week the Gunners won 7-1 at Wolves and later that season beat Sheffield United 9-2 and Blackburn 8-0.

Arsenal hit eight goals past Leicester – and it could have been nine. The referee disallowed this 'goal' by Joe Hulme for offside, but two different angles suggest that the Gunners' winger was onside.

Legendary manager Herbert Chapman after whom Arsenal's first great era was named.

The Gunners pictured early in the 1933–34 season, their second championship campaign on the run. Back row (left to right): Norman Sidey, Jim Dunne, Frank Moss, George Male, Bob John. Front row: Frank Hill, Ray Bowden, Charlie Jones, Alex James, Cliff Bastin, Eddie Hapgood.

Arsenal's new centre-forward Joe Dunne tries a shot at the Middlesbrough goal at Highbury in October 1933 but fails to score. It was Dunne's debut – he had just signed from Sheffield United – and although the new man did not mark his first appearance with a goal, the Gunners celebrated with a 6-0 win.

This time Joe Dunne did find the back of the net, scoring the only goal of the third-round FA Cup tie against Luton Town at Kenilworth Road in January 1934. Arsenal went out in the quarter-finals, at home to Aston Villa.

Arsenal put Derby County under pressure in the fifth-round FA Cup match at Highbury in February 1934. Arsenal's David Jack scored the only goal of the game.

The ball eludes Arsenal in the Cup match against Derby. It was a battle of the giants: Derby led the League championship table with the Gunners in second place.

Les Compton jumps between his goalkeeper Frank Moss and Tottenham's George Hunt at White Hart Lane in March 1935. It was a great day for the Gunners who hammered Spurs 6-0.

The champions again. Arsenal in 1934-35. Back row (left to right,: Ray Bowden, Frank Hill, Leslie Compton, Frank Moss, Tom Whittaker (trainer), Norman Sidey, Ted Drake, Jack Crayston. Front row: Joe Hulme, Pat Beasley, Cliff Bastin, George Allison (manager), Eddie Hapgood, Peter Dougall, Wilf Copping.

Ted Drake in a heading duel with a Blackburn defender and Alex James just behind them. Arsenal won this game 5-1 in October 1935.

Ted Drake scored a club record 42 goals in 41 League appearances in 1934-35. The following season Drake scored seven goals in one match alone, at Villa Park. Altogether he netted 136 goals in only 182 League and Cup games for the Gunners.

Pat Beasley of Arsenal and Billy Brown of Middlesbrough battle for possession at Highbury in December 1935. Arsenal won 2-0.

Barnsley goalkeeper Tom Ellis punches clear from an Arsenal attack at Highbury in February 1936. The Gunners, who were wearing unfamiliar hooped shirts as both teams had to change, won this FA Cup quarter-final match 4-1.

Work goes on at Highbury in April 1936 as Arsenal's Ted Drake and Chelsea's George Barber battle for a high ball. The game ended 1-1. The construction in the background is the building of the East Stand in Avenell Road which cost £130,000. It was opened six months later and accommodated over 8,000 spectators.

Arsenal in 1936, the team which won the FA Cup that year. Back row (left to right): Wilf Copping, George Male, Jack Crayston, Alex Wilson, Herbie Roberts, Ted Drake, Eddie Hapgood. Front row: George Allison (manager), Joe Hulme, Ray Bowden, Alex James, Cliff Bastin, Tom Whittaker (trainer).

Whoops! Liverpool goalkeeper Arthur Riley fumbles a shot from Alf Kirchen and Arsenal score the winning goal in the League match at Highbury in March 1937. The crowd was just over 16,000.

Arsenal in 1937-38, yet another championship-winning season. Back row (left to right): David Pryde, Ted Drake, Jack Crayston, George Swindin, Tom Whittaker (trainer), Bernard Joy, George Male, Alf Kirchen. Front row: Billy Griffiths, Ted Carr, Eddie Hapgood, George Allison (manager), George Drury, Cliff Bastin, Wilf Copping.

Derby's Jack Barker gets his arm across Cliff Bastin at Highbury in February 1938. Arsenal won 3-0.

Arsenal's new signing Bryn Jones flies into the tackle against Everton's Torry Gillick at Highbury in September 1938. Jones had recently signed from Wolves, for a record £14,000.

Everton's Alex Stevenson hits his side's first goal past George Swindin in the 14th minute. Everton scored again after Lawton hit the ball home in the 37th minute, and Arsenal eventually went down 2-1.

When war broke out in September 1939 the Football League programme was abandoned after only three matches. Eventually, properly structured regional competitions were arranged, but in the early weeks, only friendly games were allowed. On 23 September 1939, Arsenal lost such a match, 3-0 at Brentford. Here Arsenal's Reg Cumner gets the ball across as the Bees' centre-half Joe James tries to get in a tackle.

Arsenal's first wartime league game was against Charlton Athletic at White Hart Lane – Highbury had been requisitioned by the military – on 21 October 1939, a game they won 8-4 helped by four goals from Leslie Compton (three penalties) and two from his brother Denis. Here Denis Compton (11) and Charlton's Bert Turner both make a hash of heading what looks strangely like a rugby ball.

Denis Compton runs out for Arsenal just after World War Two had ended. An outside-left, Compton joined Arsenal in 1932 and made his first apperarance in the senior team in a friendly against Glasgow Rangers in September 1936. When he retired in 1950, he had made only 54 peacetime League appearances but, of course, he had lost six seasons to the war and also cricket had first call on his time; with Midldlesex and England he was one of that game's greatest names. He also made 12 wartime football appearances for England as well as 126 for Arsenal.

Joe Mercer leads out the Gunners. Wing-half Mercer was already a great name with Everton and England when he signed for Arsenal in November 1946. He retired in 1954, because of injury, having made 273 League and Cup appearances for the club. Mercer went into management, most famously in partnership with Malcolm Allison at Manchester City in the late 1960s.

Arsenal pictured in the 1948-49 season. Back row (left to right): Archie Macaulay, Wally Barnes, George Swindin, Billy Milne (trainer), Leslie Smith, Joe Mercer. Front row: Don Roper, Jimmy Logie, Ronnie Rooke, Doug Lishman, Ian McPherson, Leslie Compton. The Gunners finished fifth in Division One and went out of the FA Cup in the fourth round.

August 1948 and Manchester United are the visitors to Highbury. The Gunners' winger Ian McPherson, who had won the DFC and Bar as an RAF flying-officer, is bundled off the ball by United full-back Johnny Carey. United won 1-0 and finished runners-up, while Arsenal were fifth in the First Division.

Arsenal defender Laurie Scott is left floundering by Liverpool's Scottish international winger Billy Liddell. Nearly 56,000 saw this First Division match at Highbury in September 1949, which the Merseysiders won 2-1.

Laurie Scott (2) looks behind him as Liverpool's Willie Fagan gets in a spectacular flying header. Joe Mercer is behind Fagan.

George Swindin punches clear from a Chelsea attack during the 1950 FA Cup semi-final at White Hart Lane. The sides drew 2-2 in the first game before Arsenal won the replay 1-0 after extra-time. An aggregate of over 134,000 watched the two games.

Liverpool goalkeeper Cyril Sidlow and his defenders are in a terrible tangle during the 1950 FA Cup Final against the Gunners.

Leslie Compton hammers the ball away from Liverpool's Albert Stubbins. Arsenal's Wally Barnes and Joe Mercer are in the background.

Peter Goring is just beaten to the ball by Sidlow.

Arsenal skipper Joe
Mercer receives
the FA Cup from
King George VI
after the Gunners'
2-0 Wembley
victory over
Liverpool.

Joe Mercer is chaired by his triumphant colleagues. Because of the clash of colours, the Gunners played in unfamiliar gold-coloured shirts.

Arsenal's FA Cup-winning team of 1950. Standing (left to right): Tom Whittaker (manager), Laurie Scott, George Swindin, Wally Barnes. Seated: Denis Compton, Peter Goring, Alex Forbes, Joe Mercer, Ray Lewis, Leslie Compton. On ground: Jimmy Logie, Freddie Cox.

Leslie Compton and Liverpool's Albert Stubbins in action at Highbury in April 1951. Liverpool won 2-1 before a 42,000 crowd.

Arsenal centre-forward Cliff Holton run in as Liverpool goalkeeper Charlie Ashcroft gathers the ball safely at Highbury in September 1951. The sides drew 0-0 in front of a 50,483 crowd.

Arsenal's Doug Lishman is foiled by the bravery of Spurs's goalkeeper Ted Ditchburn.

In the same match, Cliff Holton does battle with the Tottenham defence at Highbury in September 1951. The sides drew 1-1 before a crowd of 68,164.

George Swindin tips the ball over the bar at White Hart Lane in February 1952, when nearly 67,000 saw the Gunners win 2-1.

Crowds arrive at Wembley for the 1952 FA Cup Final between Arsenal and Newcastle United. The gents' toilets appears to be doing a roaring trade.

Heads high in the Arsenal defence as Newcastle swing over a corner which is cleared.

This time it is the Gunners' turn to attack the Magpies' goal. In the end, though, it was Newcastle who triumphed, 1-0 with a goal from George Robledo.

Cliff Holton watches his shot go narrowly wide against West Brom at Highbury in March 1953. Holton and Roper scored in the 2-2 draw as Arsenal moved on their way to the League title.

Out of the Honours

Bill Dodgin of Arsenal heads clear from Dave Walsh of Aston Villa during the FA Cup third-round game at Highbury in January 1954. The Gunners won 5-1 but were then sensationally knocked out by Third Division South club Norwich City in the next round.

FA Cup action as Jack Kelsey takes the ball off the head of the Canaries' Tom Johnston. John Gavin of Norwich and Arsenal's Len Wills look on.

Norwich City's Peter Gordon beats Arsenal's Don Roper in the fourth-round tie at Highbury in January 1954, while Gunners' left-back Lionel Smith covers.

Arsenal and Spurs defenders alike seem to have missed the ball at Highbury in February 1954, when 64,211 saw the Gunners go down 3-0 to their fierce North London rivals. It was a strange season for Arsenal, who dropped to 12th place after winning the championship the previous season.

Bill Dodgin and Len Wills cannot stop Spurs winger George Robb getting across a centre. Robb scored two of Spurs' three goals that day.

Derek Tapscott, the Arsenal outside-right, gets his head to the ball as Spurs' goalkeeper Ted Ditchburn tries to punch clear with Charlie Withers of Tottenham also getting in on the action. Arsenal won 2-0 and nearly 54,000 saw the game at Highbury in September 1954.

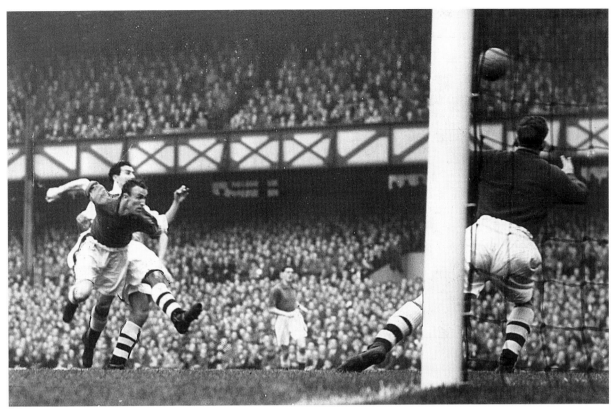

Tommy Eglington of Everton scores the only goal of the game against Arsenal at Goodison Park in August 1954. Over 69,000 saw the game, Everton's first home match since their promotion to the top flight. Jack Kelsey is the Arsenal goalkeeper.

Tapscott and Ditchburn tangle, this time at White Hart Lane in September 1955, when 51,029 saw Spurs win 3-1.

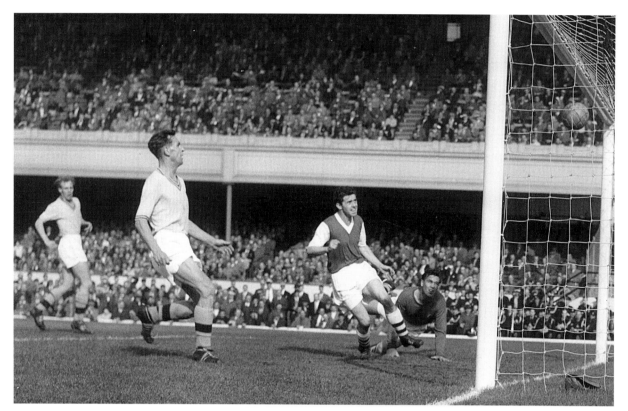

Ray Swallow scores for Arsenal against Aston Villa at Highbury in October 1957. The crowd was just over 18,000. Swallow also played first-class cricket for MCC and for Derbyshire after he joined Derby County.

Derek Tapscott gets in his shot despite the efforts of Blackpool goalkeeper George Farm at Highbury in January 1958. The Seasiders won 3-2 and the Gunners eventually slid to 12th place in the table.

In February 1958, Arsenal were involved in one of the most historic of all football matches – the last League game played by the Busby Babes before the Munich air disaster later that week. And what a thrilling match it was. At Highbury nine goals were scored before United ran out 5-4 winners. Here, United goalkeeper Harry Gregg blocks the ball as Arsenal's Jimmy Bloomfield goes tumbling. Duncan Edwards, who was to die at Munich, spreads his arms.

Jack Kelsey is ready as United attack. Tommy Taylor, another who died at Munich, is the United player on the extreme right.

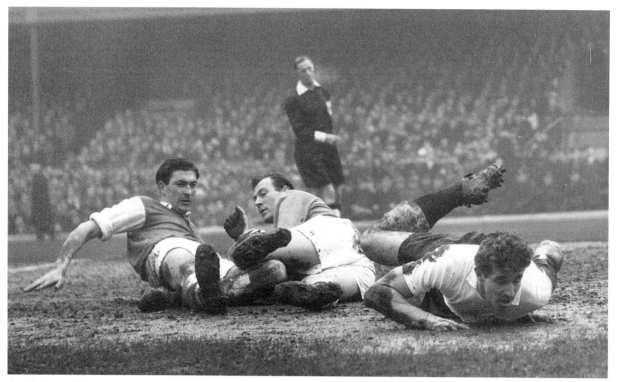

Jack Kelsey and Jim Fotheringham of Arsenal collide, and Spurs' Johnny Brooks is also floored. The game at Highbury in February 1958, watched by over 59,000 fans, ended in a 4-4 draw.

Arsenal's Jack Kelsey and Dennis Evans and Spurs' Bobby Smith all watch the flight of the ball.

Arsenal's Ray Bloomfield gets in a header from a Danny Clapton centre against Spurs at Highbury in September 1958. But the Gunners' man seems to have misdirected the ball, putting Tottenham goalkeeper John Hollowbread under no particular pressure.

John Barnwell rushes in as Preston's 16-year-old debutant goalkeeper John Barton gathers the ball at Highbury in December 1958. The youngster did well and helped his side to a 2-1 win.

Not So Swinging Sixties

Jack Kelsey dives on the ball with John Snedden and Len Wills close by against Spurs in September 1960. Spurs won 3-2.

England international forward George Eastham, seen here in action against Chelsea, joined Arsenal in November 1960, from Newcastle for £47,500, when he was 'on strike'. Eastham was in the middle of an ultimately successful legal battle against Newcastle when he challenged the retain-and-transfer system. For the Gunners he scored 41 goals in 223 senior games before being transferred to Stoke City in August 1966.

Arsenal goalkeeper John McClelland, on his debut, cannot stop Spurs' Les Allen (not in picture) from scoring at White Hart Lane in January 1961. Billy McCullough and Spurs' Cliff Jones look on. This was Spurs greatest era and they won this match 4-2.

Gordon Banks makes an acrobatic stop for Leicester City at Highbury in February 1961. Arsenal centre-forward David Herd is to the extreme right of the picture. This was a difficult time for the Gunners, who lost this game 3-1 and were again destined for midtable mediocrity.

Arsenal pictured at the start of the 1961-62 season. Back row (left to right): Ted Magill, Mel Charles, Laurie Brown, Jack Kelsey, John McClelland, Alan Skirton, Allan Young, Terry Neill. Middle row: George Swindin (manager), Danny Clapton, John Snedden, Jackie Henderson, George Eastham, Vic Groves, Billy McCullough, Geoff Strong, Dave Bacuzzi, Bertie Mee (trainer). Front row: John McLeod, Gerry Ward, Len Wills, John Petts. At the end of the season Arsenal were 10th in Division One. They went out of the FA Cup in the fourth round, to Manchester United.

Arsenal's Mel Charles heads the ball goalwards past Bradford City's Tom Flockett during the third-round FA Cup tie at Highbury in January 1962. The Gunners won 3-0, with Charles scoring two their goals, but went out 1-0 at Old Trafford in the next round.

Jack Kelsey walks back to take a goal-kick. Arsenal's Welsh international goalkeeper joined the club from junior football in 1949 and when he retired through injury in November 1962 he had played in 351 League and FA Cup games for the Gunners. He later managed the club shop at Highbury.

Welsh international Mel Charles, brother of the legendary John and father of Jeremy, who played for Swansea, QPR and Oxford, joined Arsenal in March 1959, from Swansea for £42,750 plus two reserve players. He made 64 League and FA Cup appearances before moving to Cardiff City for £28,500 in 1962.

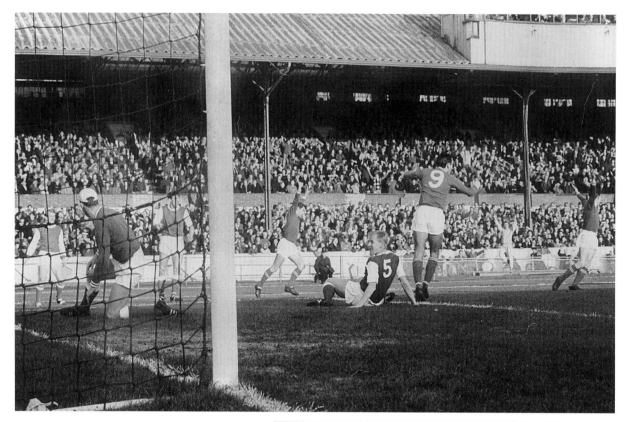

John Barnwell, goalkeeper Bob Wilson, Billy McCullough and Ian Ure are all grounded as Chelsea's Barry Bridges scores at Stamford Bridge in November 1963. Chelsea won 3-1.

Arsenal centre-half Ian Ure gets up highest against Tottenham at White Hart Lane in February 1964. The Gunners went down 3-1; earlier in the season the sides had fought out a 4-4 draw at Highbury.

Ouch! Arsenal goalkeeper Tony Burns clears a Wolves attack at Highbury in January 1965 but also collides with his own centre-half, Ian Ure. Burns, a former junior with the Gunners, made 33 appearances for them. Arsenal won this game 4-1, with a hat-trick from John Radford, his first goals for Arsenal.

Arsenal goalkeeper Jim Furnell pounces on the ball as Tottenham's Jimmy Greaves goes tumbling at White Hart Lane in September 1965. The sides drew 2-2 before a near-54,000 crowd.

Arsenal's new centre-forward George Graham, pictured just after he signed for the Gunners in September 1966, for £50,000 plus Tommy Baldwin, from Chelsea. By the time he was transferred to Manchester United in December 1972 for £120,000, Graham had scored 77 goals in 308 senior appearances. He returned to Highbury in May 1986, as manager, and soon achieved success for the Gunners.

Terry Neill (hidden) scores from the penalty spot in the 4-0 win over Spurs at Highbury in September 1967.

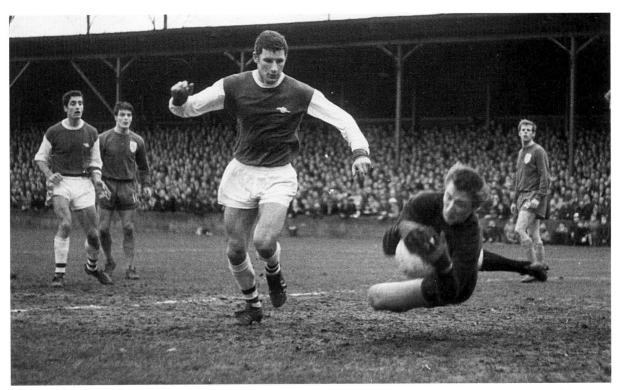

Terry Neill, who came on as a substitute for the injured John Radford, in action at Gay Meadow in January 1968, when Arsenal drew 1-1 with Shrewsbury Town in the third round of the FA Cup. The Gunners won the replay 2-0. They eventually reached the fifth round where they lost a replay at Birmingham.

On the opening day of the 1968-69 season, the Gunners won 2-1 at White Hart Lane. Here, Arsenal goalkeeper Bob Wilson makes a brave save from the feet of Spurs' debutant Jimmy Pearce. Peter Simpson (left) and Terry Neill are also in the picture.

Arsenal's David Jenkins and Liverpool's Chris Lawler both seem to have missed the ball at Highbury in August 1968. The sides drew 1–1. At the end of the season Liverpool were second, Arsenal fourth.

Arsenal reached the League Cup Final twice in the late 1960s. In the 1968 Wembley game they lost 1–0 to Leeds United. Here a scuffle develops between Ian Ure and Frank McLintock of Arsenal and Jack Charlton and Norman Hunter of Leeds. Billy Bremner appears to be acting as peacemaker.

Swindon's Roger Smart rounds Arsenal's grounded Peter Simpson before scoring his 34th-minute goal against the Gunners.

The 1969 League Cup Final saw Arsenal meet Third Division Swindon Town and a shock was in store for the Gunners, who were beaten 3-1 after extra-time. Here Bob Wilson grabs the ball from Peter Noble of Swindon as Ian Ure and Bob McNab (3) look on.

The Double-
Winning Seventies

John Roberts climbs over Nottingham Forest's Alex Ingram at Highbury in October 1970. The Gunners won 4-0 with a hat-trick from Ray Kennedy.

Peter Storey sees his header enter the Blackpool net to give Arsenal a 1-0 won over the Seasiders in March 1971 and keep the Gunners in contention for the title.

In 1970 Arsenal reached the Fairs Cup Final where they met RSC Anderlecht over two legs, losing 3-1 in Belgium but winning 3-0 at Highbury to lift the trophy on aggregate. Here the Anderlecht goalkeeper Trappeniers punches clear from Eddie Kelly at Highbury.

Trappeniers is dejected as John Radford runs past the far post after heading Arsenal's second goal. Charlie George (10) and George Armstrong are also celebrating.

Arsenal substitute Eddie Kelly scores with this spectacular effort to give Arsenal a 1-0 victory over Stoke City at Highbury in May 1971. This result left the Gunners needing to win at White Hart Lane two days later to be absolutely sure of the League championship and step towards the League and Cup double.

Arsenal players celebrate Kelly's goal as Stoke's Gordon Banks looks back in dismay.

Bob Wilson collects the ball at White Hart Lane on the last day of the 1970-71 season. Frank McLintock is sandwiched between Spurs' Alan Gilzean (right) and Martin Peters.

They did it! Arsenal won 1-0 with a header from Ray Kennedy. The final whistle has just gone and after a night of incredible tension in front of a near-52,000 crowd, the Gunners can jump for joy.

The drinks are on Ray
Kennedy, scorer of the
goal that clinched the
title. George
Armstrong and Frank
McLintock serve up
the refreshment,
which seems to be
soft drinks. The
champagne had to
wait until after the FA
Cup Final five days
later.

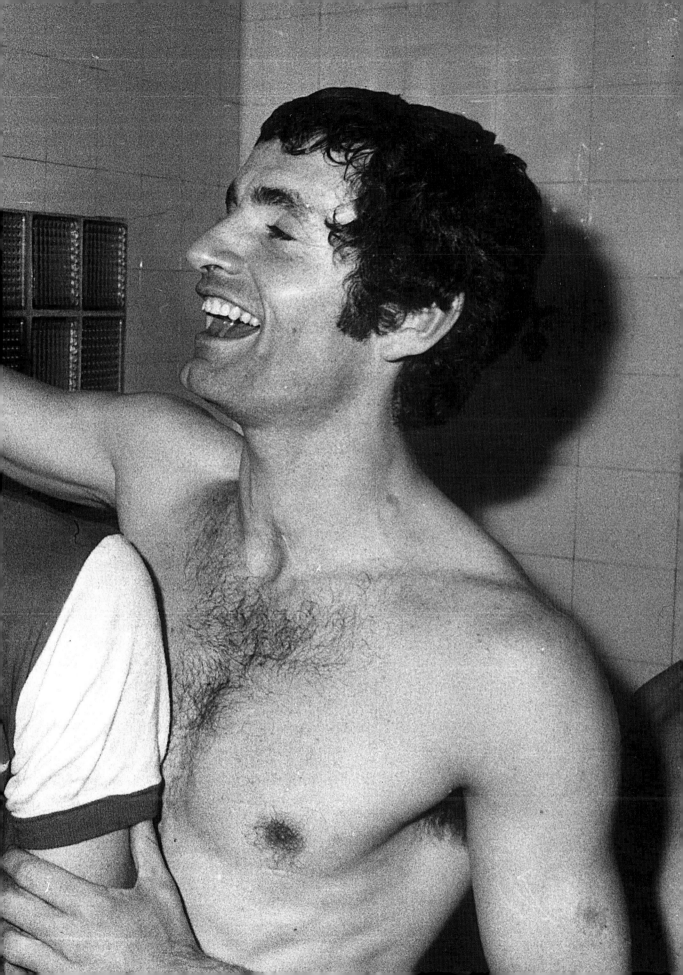

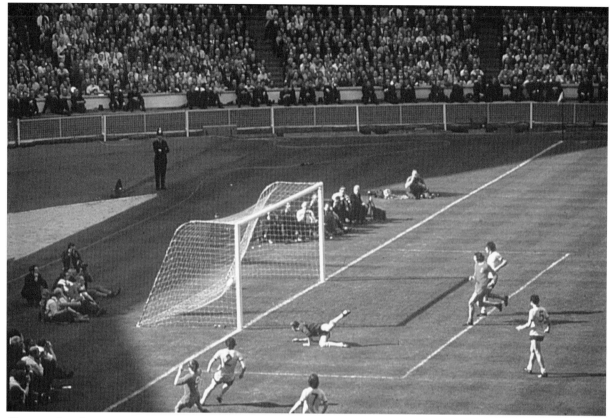

After a goalless first 90 minutes, Steve Heighway (9) puts Liverpool ahead in the 1971 FA Cup Final.

George Graham has followed up Eddie Kelly's shot and the Gunners are back on level terms. Most records credit Kelly with the goal.

Charlie George is embraced by his Arsenal teammates after scoring the winner with nine minutes of extra-time remaining in the 1971 FA Cup Final. George settled the game with a tremendous right-foot shot from 20 yards.

Arsenal skipper Frank McLintock holds aloft the FA Cup.

Arsenal's 1970-71 Double-winning squad.
Back row (left to right): Bob McNab, Ray
Kennedy, Bob Wilson, John Roberts, Geoff
Barnett, Peter Simpson, Peter Marinello.
Front row: Sammy Nelson, Peter Storey, John
Radford, Eddie Kelly, Frank McLintock, Pat
Rice, George Graham, George Armstrong.

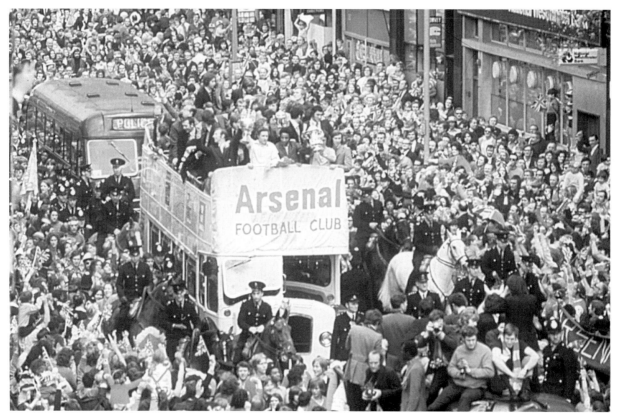

Arsenal parade their trophies around the streets of Highbury.

Ray Kennedy climbs high to head goalwards during the Gunners' 4-0 victory over Norwegian champions Stromgodset at Highbury in September 1971. Arsenal won the first-round European Cup tie 7-1 on aggregate.

Frank McLintock watches as John Radford and a Grasshoppers Zurich defender perform an aerial ballet at Highbury in the 1971-72 European Cup second-round. Arsenal won the tie 5-0 on aggregate.

Peter Storey battles past a Grasshoppers defender. In the quarter-finals the Gunners lost 2-1 in Holland to Ajax Amsterdam and could not pull that around in the second leg at Highbury, where they lost 1-0.

Ray Kennedy gets a high ball under control despite the attentions of Nottingham Forest's Dave Serella at Highbury in April 1972. The Gunners won 3-0.

Arsenal's reserve goalkeeper Geoff Barnett, standing in for the injured Bob Wilson, is beaten by a header from Leeds United's Allan Clarke in the 1972 FA Cup Final at Wembley. It proved to be the only goal of the game.

The race is on between Arsenal's colourful winger Peter Marinello and Liverpool's Steve Heighway at Highbury in September 1972. Over 47,000 saw a goalless draw. At the end of the season Liverpool were champions, Arsenal runners-up three points behind.

Coventry City goalkeeper Bill Glazier punches the ball away from Arsenal's George Graham at Highbury in November 1972. The Midlands side scored a surprise 2-0 win in what was Graham's last appearance for the Gunners.

Charlie George seems to be the one with his eye on the ball as he is surrounded by Everton defenders at Highbury in November 1972.
John Radford scored the only goal of the game.

Jeff Blockley is sandwiched between Stoke City defenders at Highbury in September 1973. The Gunners won 2-1.

In January 1974, Arsenal drew 1-1 with Aston Villa in the fourth round of the FA Cup but lost the Villa Park replay 2-0. Here a relieved Pat Rice and Bob Wilson watch the ball go out for a goal-kick at Highbury.

Villa's Ian Hamilton heads goalwards past Jeff Blockley and Pat Rice.

John Radford and Mike England do battle at Highbury in February 1974. Spurs won 1-0.

April 1974 and Alan Ball is the object of close attention from Derby County's Bruce Rioch. Charlie George, later to join Derby, looks on. The Gunners won this game at Highbury 2-0, with Ball, from the penalty spot, and George the scorers.

West Ham's Billy Jennings gets in a header at Highbury in October 1974. Eddie Kelly, Terry Mancini and John Radford are the Arsenal players. The Gunners won 3-0.

Arsenal goalkeeper Jimmy Rimmer slides into Stoke's Geoff Hurst at Highbury in March 1975. John Matthews and Pat Rice look on. The game ended 1-1.

Liverpool's Kevin Keegan gets between Peter Simpson and Terry Mancini at Highbury in February 1975. The Gunners won 2-0, both goals coming from Alan Ball, one of them from the penalty spot.

Arsenal's Brian Kidd and Terry Mancini look on anxiously as their goalkeeper Jimmy Rimmer punches away from Liverpool's Phil Thompson. The Arsenal number seven is George Armstrong.

West Ham visited Highbury twice in the 1974-75 season, winning 2-0 in an FA Cup quarter-final match there in March. Brian Kidd and the Hammers' Kevin Lock are both airborne. West Ham went on to win the Cup that year.

Arsenal pictured in at the start of the 1975-76 season. Back row (left to right): Bobby Campbell (coach), Brian Horsby, Terry Mancini, John Matthews, Jimmy Rimmer, Brian Kidd, Geoff Barnett, Trevor Ross, Richard Powling, Wilf Rostron, Fred Street (physiotherapist). Front row: Pat Rice, Alex Cropley, Sammy Nelson, Eddie Kelly, John Radford, Berti Mee (manager), Alan Ball, Peter Storey, Peter Simpson, George Armstrong, Liam Brady. It was a poor campaign for the Gunners – 17th in Division One and out of both the FA and League Cups at the first hurdle.

Manchester United's Stewart Houston gets the better of Liam Brady at Highbury in November 1975. The Gunners won 3-1.

Frank Stapleton heads Arsenal's goal against Ipswich Town at Highbury in April 1976. It was the Suffolk club who emerged winners, however, 2–1. George Burley of Ipswich and Alex Cropley are in the background.

Everton's Roger Kenyon leans on Arsenal centre-forward Malcolm Macdonald while the Gunners' Richey Powling misses the ball at Highbury in September 1976.

Powling heads clear again as Frank Stapleton and Everton's Ken McNaught go flying. The Gunners won 3-1.

Former Arsenal player Ray Kennedy, now playing for Liverpool, shields the ball from the Gunners' Trevor Ross at Highbury in November 1976. The game ended 1-1.

Malcolm Macdonald, scorer of the game's only goal, is tackled by David Needham of Queen's Park Rangers at Highbury in October 1977.

Bristol City v Arsenal is a rare League fixture but in 1977–78 the Ashton Gate club were in the top flight and in October they lost 2-0 at home to the Gunners. Here Pat Jennings punches clear from a City corner.

David O'Leary hammers Arsenal's third goal against Chelsea at Highbury on Boxing Day 1977, with goalkeeper Peter Bonetti grounded. The Gunners won 3-0.

Malcolm Macdonald wheels away in joy after scoring Arsenal's first goal against Manchester United at Highbury in April 1978. Macdonald scored again as the Gunners won 3-1.

Orient's Peter Bennett fails to stop a shot from David Price of Arsenal in the 1978 FA Cup semi-final at Stamford Bridge, which the Gunners won 3-0.

Graham Rix finishes off a solo run to score Arsenal's third goal against Orient. John Jackson is the stranded goalkeeper.

Goalkeeper Pat Jennings is beaten by Paul Mariner's shot in the 1978 FA Cup Final but the Ipswich man's effort hit the woodwork. Nevertheless, the Suffolk club won 1-0.

Frank Stapleton gets in a shot as Ipswich's Kevin Beattie launches a tackle. Future Ipswich manager George Burley is the player to the right of the picture.

The following season, in the First Division, Arsenal gained some revenge by beating Ipswich 4-1 at Highbury. Frank Stapleton watches his shot go in for his second goal of the match. Stapleton went on to complete his hat-trick.

A crowded Middlesbrough goalmouth at Highbury in February 1979. 'Boro goalkeeper Jim Stewart punches clear from Frank Stapleton and Willie Young. His defenders are McAndrew, Ashcroft and Boam. The game ended 0-0.

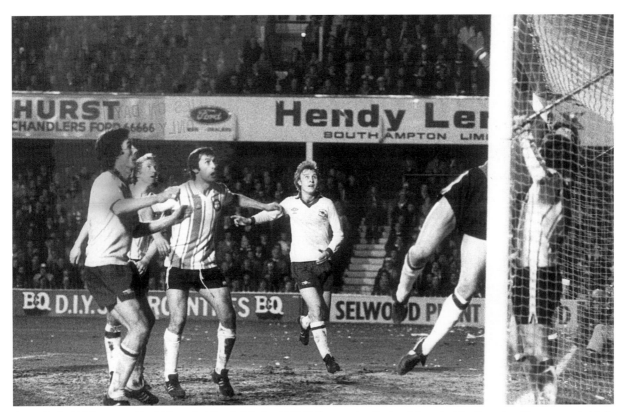

Arsenal's David Price scores his side's goal at The Dell in the 1979 FA Cup quarter-final match against Southampton. The game ended 1-1 and Arsenal won the replay 2-0.

Alan Sunderland scores Arsenal's second goal in the 1979 FA Cup semi-final against Wolves at Villa Park where 46,244 saw the Gunners win 2-0.

The 1979 FA Cup Final between Arsenal and Manchester United only came to life in the last five minutes. Arsenal had seemed to be coasting to a 2-0 win when United scored twice in quick succession to draw level. Then, when extra-time seemed certain, Alan Sunderland scored the winner. Here, United's Lou Macari tries an overhead kick but the ball cleared Pat Rice, Pat Jennings and the Arsenal crossbar. Young looks on.

Brian Talbot and Alan Sunderland arrive at the same time but it is Talbot who is adjudged to have put the Gunners 1-0 ahead. Buchan and Coppell are the two United players.

Victorious Arsenal with the FA Cup after their sensational last-gasp winner against Manchester United in the 1979 Final.

Steve Walford pushes the ball to Liam Brady as Leeds United's Terry Connor closes in at Highbury in January 1980. Leeds won 1-0.

Frank Stapleton (9) and David Price, together with Derby's David Webb, are frozen in an acrobatic tableau at Highbury in January 1980. Arsenal won 2-0. Stapleton later played for Derby.

Frank Stapleton is performing acrobatics again, this time against Aston Villa. Arsenal won this game at Highbury in February 1980 by 3-1. The Villa players are Allan Evans (4) and Ken McNaught (5).

February 1980 and Bolton goalkeeper Jim McDonagh scrambles the ball away as his defender Mike Walsh tries to hold off Frank Stapleton. The Gunners won 2-0, having a few days earlier knocked Bolton out of the FA Cup after a replay.

Alan Sunderland scores Arsenal's first goal of the 1979-80 FA Cup campaign,
in the replay against Cardiff City at Highbury. The first game ended goalless
but Arsenal won the second match 2-1, Sunderland scoring both goals.

And the Cup road ended at Wembley... David O'Leary hammers the ball clear from a West Ham United attack in the 1980 FA Cup Final. O'Leary's Arsenal teammate Willie Young is on the left of the picture. The Hammers won 1-0 with a rare headed goal from Trevor Brooking.